HISTORY OF ROCK BANDS

Scott Witmer

VISIT US AT
WWW.ABDOPUBLISHING.COM

Published by ABDO Publishing Company, 8000 West 78th Street, Suite 310, Edina, MN 55439. Copyright ©2010 by Abdo Consulting Group, Inc. International copyrights reserved in all countries. No part of this book may be reproduced in any form without written permission from the publisher. ABDO & Daughters™ is a trademark and logo of ABDO Publishing Company.

Printed in the United States.

 PRINTED ON RECYCLED PAPER

Editor: John Hamilton
Graphic Design: Sue Hamilton
Cover Design: John Hamilton
Cover Photo: Corbis
Interior Photos and Illustrations: AP-pgs 12 & 13; Corbis-pgs 4, 5, 11, 16, 18, 20, 21, 22, 24, & 26; Getty Images-pgs 7, 8, 9, 10, 14, 15, 17, 19, 22, 23, 25, 27, 28, & 29; iStockphoto-pgs 1 & 3; and Jupiterimages-pg 3.

Library of Congress Cataloging-in-Publication Data

Witmer, Scott.
   History of rock bands / Scott Witmer.
      p. cm. -- (Rock band)
   Includes index.
   ISBN 978-1-60453-692-8
   1. Rock music--History and criticism--Juvenile literature. 2. Rock groups--Juvenile literature. I. Title.
   ML3534.W614 2009
   781.66--dc22
                              2009006609

CONTENTS

WHY WE LOVE ROCK BANDS

Rock Bands are an important part of pop culture. They are featured in magazines, television, and movies. Why are they so popular? Is it the money, the fashions, or the lavish lifestyles? For the most part, the reason for the intense interest is a love of music.

Almost every band is formed because its members want to write, create, and perform music. Whether heavy metal, techno, or emo, bands get together because they want to explore the music they love. Even though some bands become famous for their "rock star" behavior, it is the love of music that inspired them to become musicians in the first place.

Many bands also want to express their opinions through the music they play. U2 is famous for the socially charged songs they write. Bob Marley and the Wailers wrote and performed songs about the injustices they witnessed in their home country of Jamaica. Whatever the opinion or cause, rock musicians often combine their messages with unforgettable music to create art that lasts for decades.

> Bob Marley and the Wailers performed Jamaican reggae songs about the injustices they witnessed. Marley died of cancer in 1981, but his music and popularity have increased through the years. *Time* magazine named the group's album *Exodus* as the greatest album of the 20th century.

Lead singer Bono and the entire U2 rock band are famous for both their music and their work promoting human rights.

THE 1950s

There are many stories about the beginnings of rock and roll. The stories overlap each other, and it is hard to tell what is fact and what is exaggerated legend. For example, it is unlikely that Robert Johnson, the "Grandfather of Rock 'n' Roll," actually sold his soul to the devil in exchange for his guitar skills. Yet, it is these types of stories that help keep the world intrigued by rock music, and the bands that play it.

Rock and roll music is a fusion of several primarily American styles of music. The influences of rhythm and blues, country, bluegrass, gospel, folk, and jazz music can all be heard. The use of the electronically amplified guitar became the defining feature of this new musical style. The electric guitar remains a crucial element of rock and roll music today.

In the 1950s, rock was first defined by bands that performed with one or more guitars, a drum set, and a bass guitar. Pianos and saxophones were also common in rock bands of the 1950s. The style fused the upbeat parts of blues and country music with a distinct beat and a very simple pop song structure. Rock and roll became very popular in America, and quickly spread around the globe.

Although the term "rock and roll" had been used in several rhythm and blues songs of the 1940s, the phrase is usually credited to Cleveland, Ohio, disc jockey Alan Freed. In the early 1950s, Freed hosted a radio show that played a mix of musical styles, including rhythm and blues, gospel, and country. He described this new blend of music as rock and roll, and the name stuck.

A 45 rpm record from popular rock and roll artist Bo Diddley.

Elvis Presley and his backup singers, the Jordanaires, appeared on the *Ed Sullivan Show* on October 28, 1956. More than 60 million people watched Presley's performance on their TVs. Only 21 years old, Presley was on his way to becoming "The King of Rock and Roll."

Many music historians credit Elvis Presley with recording the first rock and roll record, "That's All Right (Mama)," for Sun Records in Memphis, Tennessee, in 1954. However, some people date the first rock records back as early as the end of the 1800s. But no matter who came first, popular history credits Elvis with bringing rock music to the general public. He grew to become a phenomenally popular artist, and was dubbed "The King of Rock and Roll."

In the 1950s, other important rock and roll bands included Bill Haley and His Comets, Muddy Waters, The Platters, and The Everly Brothers. Several solo acts also advanced the rock musical style in the 50s, including Big Joe Turner, Little Richard, Chuck Berry, Bo Diddley, Fats Domino, and many others.

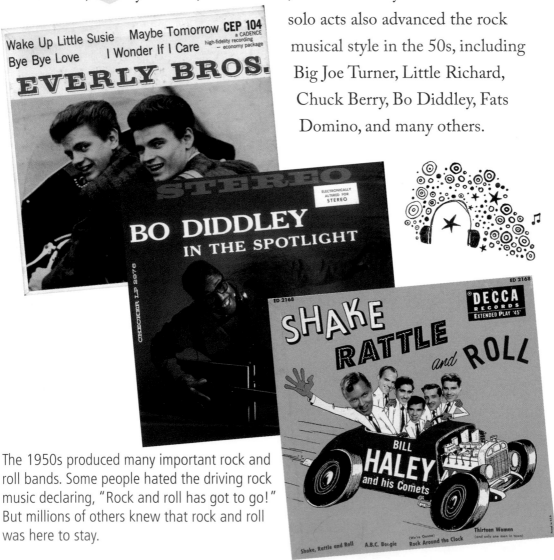

The 1950s produced many important rock and roll bands. Some people hated the driving rock music declaring, "Rock and roll has got to go!" But millions of others knew that rock and roll was here to stay.

> Bill Haley and His Comets came together in 1952. The band was one of the earliest groups to bring rock and roll to the attention of America. Their hit song, "Rock Around the Clock," came out in 1954. It slowly climbed the charts, reaching number one, where it stayed for eight weeks. It is estimated that 25 million copies of the song have been sold.

THE 1960s

During the early 1960s, rock and roll became wildly popular in England. This ushered in an era called the "British invasion." On February 9, 1964, The Beatles performed in America for the first time on *The Ed Sullivan Show*. Beatlemania was born as Americans snatched up records by the group. The music, clothes, and hairstyles of The Beatles became an obsession, paving the way for other English bands to achieve success in America. During this time, rock bands such as The Byrds, The Rolling Stones, and The Animals all found success in the United States.

In the late 60s and early 70s, rock began a transformation. The cleaner, rhythm-and-blues sounds of early rock were transformed to a fuzzier, harder electric sound. "Psychedelic" bands began to spring up on the West Coast of the United States. The Doors, The Grateful Dead, The Velvet Underground, and Jefferson Airplane all were pioneers of this kind of music. The psychedelic sound spread to England, influencing such bands as Pink Floyd and the Moody Blues.

> From August 15-18, 1969, the largest outdoor rock concert was held in upstate New York. Woodstock featured many excellent musicians, including Jimi Hendrix, seen here on stage. No one knows exactly how many people attended Woodstock, but it was estimated at 400,000.

The Rolling Stones are one of the bands from England that achieved great success in America.

> Paul McCartney, John Lennon, Ringo Starr, and George Harrison were all from Liverpool, England. The group came together in 1962 after Starr took the place of former drummer Pete Best.

In 1957, as American rock and roll was gaining popularity around the world, John Lennon and some friends formed a band called The Quarry Men in their hometown of Liverpool, England. John was introduced to guitarist Paul McCartney, who soon joined the band.

The following year, Paul's college friend George Harrison asked John to let him in the band. Lennon eventually agreed, and three-fourths of The Beatles' legendary lineup was in place. The band toured around small clubs in Europe, using different drummers. Their name changed several times. Eventually, after landing a record contract with EMI Records, the band was joined by drummer Ringo Starr. They also settled on a new name— The Beatles.

> Before coming up with their name, The Beatles performed under the names The Quarry Men, Johnny and the Moondogs, the Beatals, the Silver Beetles, the Silver Beats, and the Silver Beatles. It's said that the Beatles name was a variation on the popular group Buddy Holly and the Crickets, changing the spelling of "beetle" to reflect the strong BEAT in their songs.

> On August 15, 1965, The Beatles performed for more than 55,000 screaming fans at Shea Stadium in Flushing, New York. Beatlemania was at its height. The noise was so loud, none of the band members could hear each other. At one point, John Lennon began playing the keyboard with his elbows, amusing the other band members.

The Beatles recorded several singles in the early 1960s. Their first record was "Love Me Do," which was released in 1962. The band enjoyed success in England, with several number-one records.

In February 1964, The Beatles performed a historic gig on *The Ed Sullivan Show*. Almost overnight, the band became a sensation in the United States, and the world. "Beatlemania" was born, and the group quickly became the best-selling rock band in history. The Beatles broke many sales and chart-position records, many of which still stand today.

For the next six years, The Beatles released an avalanche of classic albums, including *Revolver*, *Magical Mystery Tour*, *Sgt. Pepper's Lonely Hearts Club Band*, and *Abbey Road*. They performed many historic concerts, and also released successful movies, including 1964's *A Hard Day's Night* and 1965's *Help!* The Beatles were also the first true "stadium rock" band, performing in a stadium built for sports, New York's Shea Stadium, in 1965.

By the late 1960s, after years of phenomenal success, the members of The Beatles began to have creative differences. Continuous squabbles and disagreements eventually led to the band's demise. In April 1970, the band announced their breakup, and The Beatles were no more.

All four members enjoyed solo success after The Beatles. On December 8, 1980, John Lennon, a man who had preached a life of peace and non-violence, was murdered in front of his home in New York City. And in 2001, George Harrison died of cancer. Paul McCartney and Ringo Starr continue making music to this day.

Many musicians and music historians insist that The Beatles were the most important rock band in history. They created songs that are timeless, which continue to influence today's popular artists. The Beatles' influence can be seen in almost every facet of rock and roll. Their movies paved the way for modern music videos. Their creative vision on such classic albums as *Sgt. Pepper's Lonely Heart's Club Band* remains inspirational to every artist today who seeks to push the limits of what can be created with music.

Countless bands have followed in The Beatles' footsteps, building on their songwriting style of melody and substance. The Beatles' helped bring rock and roll as we know it to the world. Their influence can be traced to virtually every rock band in existence today.

THE 1970s

In the 1970s, rock and roll began to evolve, and several sub-genres of the music were created. Some bands embraced country and folk music, such as The Eagles. Others continued to make heavier rock music, creating a genre called hard rock. Hard rock continued the trend towards more aggressive, electrically distorted rock music. This music was played by such classic artists as KISS, Led Zeppelin, Aerosmith, and Van Halen. These bands furthered the use of a lead guitar in rock, with skillful, blistering electric guitar solos.

In the late 1970s, several bands pushed the envelope of hard rock and created a style called punk. Punk rock was heavy, fast, and dealt with themes of questioning authority and conformity. The Sex Pistols from England are credited with ushering in this phenomenon. They were loud, fast, crude, and questioned all societal norms. Their songs were short, simple, and furious. They quickly gained a large following in England, and then worldwide. Along with The Sex Pistols, The Clash was another English punk band at the time. While not as rebellious as the Sex Pistols, The Clash performed socially conscious punk music that was fused with a reggae sound. In America, The Ramones and The New York Dolls led the punk music charge.

> The Clash on their 1979 American tour. From left to right: Joe Strummer, Topper Headon, Paul Simonon, and Mick Jones.

Aerosmith members Brad Whitford, Tom Hamilton, Steven Tyler, Joey Kramer (drums), and Joe Perry performed on *The Midnight Special* at NBC Studios in Burbank, California, in 1974.

> The English rock band Led Zeppelin formed in 1968. It included band members Jimmy Page (guitar), Robert Plant (vocals), John Paul Jones (bass guitar, keyboards), and John Bonham (drums).

In 1968, English guitarist Jimmy Page was playing in a blues-rock band called The Yardbirds, with Eric Clapton and Jeff Beck. When Clapton and Beck left to pursue other musical endeavors, Page had to rebuild the band. He hired John Paul Jones as bass guitarist and keyboardist, Robert Plant as vocalist, and John Bonham on the drums. Legend has it that a skeptical Keith Moon, drummer for The Who, said the new band would "go down like a lead zeppelin." After removing the "a" in "lead" so nobody would mispronounce it "leed," Led Zeppelin was born.

Led Zeppelin's sound was influenced by American blues music. The band injected a heavier, distorted guitar sound, making it one of the first heavy metal acts. Led Zeppelin released many successful albums worldwide. In 1971, the band released their fourth album, which was unnamed. Instead, it had four strange symbols on the cover. It is often simply called *The Fourth Album*. Many critics say it is one of the greatest rock albums of all time. The most famous track from the album is the Grammy Hall of Fame Award winner "Stairway to Heaven."

Led Zeppelin rose to superstardom in the 1970s. The band members became famous for their "rock star" antics. They flew in private jets, rented entire floors of hotels, and, reportedly, destroyed hotel rooms and backstage areas. Led Zeppelin had a reputation for rock and roll excess, although the band members, plus other sources, agree that most of the stories about their adventures were exaggerated.

Led Zeppelin continued to release successful albums until 1980. In September of that year, drummer John Bonham was found dead of asphyxiation. Drinking too much alcohol was probably the cause. After the tragedy, the remaining members of Led Zeppelin decided to disband.

Led Zeppelin was one of the most influential rock bands to ever play. Several current alternative rock bands emulate the "Zeppelin sound" of the mid-1970s. Even though they are known for heavy metal, Led Zeppelin was perhaps the most versatile commercially successful band ever. They continually transformed their sound, infusing blues, country, reggae, and folk into the albums they created. Led Zeppelin's albums remain relevant and timeless today.

In 2007, Led Zeppelin reunited for a one-night tribute show for Ahmet Ertegun, the Atlantic Records executive who had originally signed the band in 1968. Ertegun had died in a fall in 2006. The show took place at the O2 Arena in London, England, on December 10, 2007.

THE 1980s

I n the late 1970s and early 1980s, musicians began combining punk and popular music with electronic instruments. The synthesizer keyboard became a popular instrument. It was capable of transforming sounds in virtually limitless ways. This music was called New Wave in America.

New Wave was a stark contrast to the popular disco dance movement that had become popular at the time. At first, the term New Wave described bands with punk roots but with a more "pop music," radio-friendly sound, such as The Police, or Elvis Costello. Later, the term was used to describe bands with heavy electronic elements. New Wave artists such as The Cars, Blondie, Talking Heads, and Devo all wrote rock songs with an electronic feel.

The New Wave movement created several sub-genres. Industrial was electronic music that used hard rock's aggressive song structure and production. Important industrial bands included Ministry, Skinny Puppy, and more recently, Nine Inch Nails. Goth was electronically influenced music that featured dark tones and lyrics that could range from emotional to gloomy. The Cure, Bauhaus, Siouxie and the Banshees, and The Joy Division are popular examples of Goth bands.

Blondie

Devo

> The Police were a British rock trio made up of Stewart Copeland (drums, percussion, vocals), Sting (lead vocals, bass guitar), and Andy Summers (guitar, vocals). They used a combination of rock, post-punk, reggae, and New Wave styles. *Rolling Stone* magazine named The Police number 70 on their list of the 100 Greatest Artists of All Time.

I Want My MTV

In 1981, a new cable television channel was launched. This young station featured videos and news of popular music. The channel was called Music Television, or MTV. MTV changed the way that music was marketed to consumers forever. Music was taken out of the radio and thrust into the living room. MTV continues to be a driving force for music sales, even today.

During the 1980s, an offshoot of hard rock evolved into glam metal bands. They were sometimes called hair bands because of the performers' long and teased up locks, plus the use of heavy makeup. Hair bands usually performed hard rock music with a harder, heavier-driving style. The lead guitars were more prominent, and the stage theatrics were more extravagant. Poison, Mötley Crüe, and Twisted Sister were early examples of glam metal bands. They were followed by countless other glam metal bands throughout the 1980s. Proving the popularity of these bands, Quiet Riot's *Metal Health* album in 1983 was the first heavy metal album to ever reach number one on America's Billboard charts.

R.E.M.

Depeche Mode

During the 1980s, bands that did not play metal, or pop, or any other easily categorized music were lumped into a category called alternative rock. These bands enjoyed a large growth in the 80s because of college radio play, plus the increasing growth of independent record labels. Alternative music was truly a catch-all classification. Bands as diverse as R.E.M., Depeche Mode, The Cure, The Pixies, Jane's Addiction, and The Replacements were all included as alternative bands, despite their vast differences in sound. By the late 80s, alternative bands embraced and expanded the punk, Goth, and industrial movements started a decade earlier.

> Hard rock band
Mötley Crüe was
made up of Nikki Sixx,
Mick Mars, Vince Neil,
and Tommy Lee.

23

THE 1990s

In 1991, Seattle-based Nirvana released their second album, *Nevermind*. Nirvana's music was a type of alternative music called grunge. It was a darker, heavier type of guitar rock that originated in the American Northwest, especially the Seattle, Washington, area. Often called the Seattle Sound, grunge was well known for the loud-soft-loud song structure, in which verses were soft, and choruses raged loudly. *Nevermind* was a huge commercial success. Glam metal and pop bands were suddenly not "cool" anymore, and alternative music dominated mainstream radio. In the 90s, alternative rock became so popular that it was no longer really alternative. Other grunge bands quickly rose to the top of the charts, including Pearl Jam, Alice in Chains, and Soundgarden.

> Eddie Vedder sings, while guitarist Stone Gossard and bass player Jeff Ament jam behind him, during a Pearl Jam concert in September 1993.

In the 1990s, the explosion of alternative music spawned several other musical genres. Riot Grrrl is a post-punk type of music played primarily by female bands. They rebelled against the male-dominated music industry, with feminist themes and aggressive songwriting. Riot Grrrl bands included Bikini Kill, Hole, and Sleater-Kinney.

The late 90s also produced a genre called nu-metal, which was heavy metal music with a hip-hop influence. Bands like Rage Against the Machine, Limp Bizkit, Korn, and Linkin Park fused a driving metal beat with rap-like lyrics.

In Great Britain, bands like Oasis returned to the melodic songwriting of the 1960s, with a modern rock influence. Called Britpop, it was an alternative to the depressing grunge sound coming from America. Bands like Blur and Radiohead were also driving forces behind the Britpop sound.

The "Madchester Sound," named for the town of Manchester, England, produced bands that fused alternative rock with dance music. These trendsetters included New Order, The Happy Mondays, and The Stone Roses.

NIRVANA

> Kurt Cobain, Krist Novoselic, and Dave Grohl of the grunge band Nirvana. The band, and their darker rock music, originated in their home state of Washington.

In 1987, two friends from Aberdeen, Washington, decided to start a band. Guitarist Kurt Cobain and bassist Krist Novoselic formed what eventually became the grunge band Nirvana. They released an album with then-drummer Chad Channing, with modest success. Channing left the band, and drummer Dave Grohl was hired. In 1990, Nirvana signed with DGC Records, and began recording the historic album *Nevermind*.

When *Nevermind* was released, the record label had low expectations for success. However, the single "Smells Like Teen Spirit" propelled the album to a number-one spot in America, and in many other countries around the world. Suddenly, this "underground grunge" band was thrust into the spotlight, much to the dissatisfaction of the reclusive Kurt Cobain. The band released just two more studio albums before Cobain's untimely death in 1994.

Nirvana brought alternative music to the spotlight. The success of *Nevermind* was a game changer for the entire music industry. Suddenly, record companies were trying to sign every band on college radio. Mainstream radio stations were playing alternative music, and the public was buying it.

The record companies had to find a new way of doing business in the post-Nirvana world. Previously, record companies would put an act together and push it on the buying public. After the success of Nirvana, record companies began more actively searching out bands with built-in fan bases to sign. Not only did Nirvana change the way that record companies did business, the band also changed the landscape of modern popular music. Alternative became mainstream, and more accepted. Even today, the airwaves are dominated by alternative music. Every band since 1991 that has enjoyed success as an alternative act has Nirvana to thank.

> Lead singer Kurt Cobain found success, and the accompanying attention, difficult to manage. Tragically, he was found dead of a self-inflicted gunshot wound in his Seattle, Washington, home in April 1994.

THE 2000s

As rock bands turned the corner into the 21st century, the music that they produced was becoming more and more diverse. Bands today draw influences from the half-century of rock music that came before them. Garage bands like the White Stripes and The Gossip revived the fuzzy lo-fi sound of the 1970s. Emo bands like Dashboard Confessional, Thursday, and My Chemical Romance mix punk rock and thematic songwriting with emotional, expressive lyric styles. British bands Franz Ferdinand and Bloc Party continue the British tradition of indie songwriting with a rhythm suited to dancing.

As long as there are people willing to pick up instruments, start a band, and write music, there can be no limit to the styles of music that will be created in the future.

> Lead singer Kele Okereke of the band Bloc Party performs on November 25, 2008 in Sydney, Australia.

Meg White and Jack White of the White Stripes have revived the fuzzy lo-fi sound of the 1970s.

GLOSSARY

ALTERNATIVE MUSIC

A style of music that is unlike the current mainstream music. In the 1990s, several alternative rock bands, each with their own unique sound, became popular with fans looking for something different.

BEATLEMANIA

A frenzied interest in the 1960s rock group, The Beatles. Fan clubs arose for the group as a whole, as well as for John Lennon, Paul McCartney, George Harrison, and Ringo Starr individually. Their images were placed on everything from posters to lunch boxes. Plus, the group's music, clothing, hairstyles, and interests were closely watched and mimicked.

BILLBOARD CHARTS

A reporting of music sales, radio airplay, and numbered rankings by *Billboard* magazine. People pay close attention to *Billboard's* weekly top 10 list of songs and albums.

BRITISH INVASION

A time when groups from Great Britain became wildly popular in the United States. The term usually refers to the 1960s, and the popularity of The Beatles, The Rolling Stones, and other British rock groups in America.

DISCO

A popular dance music with a strong bass beat. Disco was commonly heard in the 1970s.

Gig

A job as a musician.

New Wave

A genre of 1980s rock that mixed punk and popular music, and often used electronic instruments such as synthesizer keyboards.

Pop Culture

Short for popular culture. The most popular music, entertainment, foods, and styles of a specific point in time in a specific country.

> Singer Axl Rose and guitarist Slash perform on stage with the rock band Guns N' Roses. Their song "Welcome to The Jungle" was named the number-one greatest hard rock song by VH1.

INDEX